Let the black dog follow

Gemma Wilkie

Presentation by *BookLeaf Publishing*

Web: www.bookleafpub.com

E-mail: info@bookleafpub.com

ISBN: 9789357616676

First edition 2022

To those closest that kept my head above water

And to the shrinking violets out there that are anything but

ACKNOWLEDGEMENT

To the awe-inspiring, eloquent poets out there who I'll never measure up to. Thank you for keeping me sane over lockdown.

PREFACE

I've spent the majority of my adult life maintaining a comfortable volume. Careful to never rock the boat too much, overly offend anyone and keep the peace. I've not had much experience of being in a space where I've felt encouraged to be loud and outrageous. Now in my late twenties i'm realising just how dangerous that is.

And I think it's about time we start making noise.

This little book touches upon all matters of life, from heartbreak and finding oneself, to mental health and healing, to our biggest fears and the fragility of time.

I hope this speaks to anyone that has gone through any morsel of pain during their time on earth. Us silly humans have a tendency to compare trauma and sometimes brush experiences under the rug as someone else always 'has it worse than me'.

Pain is not a measuring tape.

I read somewhere that going through any kind of trauma is like standing on your own personal island and you can see others on their island waving back. But what links these islands, that are all different shapes and sizes, are bridges to one another. Ultimately connecting us all and our collective experiences. And when I read that I thought that was beautifully explained. That you'll never be alone. And even if you have the, 'that's life' mentality, which I very much do, the impact of someone saying 'Hey, that wasn't easy what you went through. Recognise that.', is just a game changer. Makes you take a beat, set boundaries and look after yourself.

So if there was anything I'd love someone reading this little book to take away, it would be to recognise that your truth is important, your voice vital and your strength is nothing short of beautiful.

When it hits you

I once had a conversation with a friend
We were at a party
Sitting outside at the edge,
Looking across at the chaos
I said, I worry i'm going to miss it
They looked at me,
Miss what?
I didn't blink,
Everything

Guilt

After the waves settle
Still waters all but remain
Shame and longing flood in
Drifting me off to sleep

The answer doesn't change anything

Dizzy thinking of
Why you are the way you are
What's the point?

Crossroads

What more can be done
The starless night has taken you

No,
You've let it

Woosh, winded,
Legs buckled
Body limp

It's too dark to see,
Rainbow pixels dancing
To the tune of ebbing

All the while
I'm straining to reach you
Knuckles white
The dirt and stones digging in

Now I see nothing
And the crescendo has long past
The outro nearing

Honey, I'm tired
I know

My knees hurt
It's okay
And I can't feel you anymore
So let go

Biggest Fear

Here on my deathbed
With surmountable regret,
Because I said 'no'

I miss you

You filled my life with music,
It's too quiet now

Let them see

Shoulders back, chin high
Put your phone away,
Meet people in the eye
No fidget fingers, your belly fire-lit
Remember,
You are anything but a shrinking violet

Single

You saw my cover
And made your judgment
I want her, you thought
A surface level lover

Traced the curve of my spine,
Licked fingers
Thumbing through pages
Nothing here but sunshine

Skimreading

Seconds of bitter sweet
You tasted the salt from my skin,
Honey dew between and
Decided there's nothing here within

I pity you,
For everything you didn't factor
You had a library of wonder
And chose to read but one chapter

Insecure

People will settle for anything
Just so they can say they have something

I'll be damned if I let this happen

Media

We pick apart pieces of ourselves

Round off the rough edges and
Buffer out the creases

Each with our own first aid box
Plastering smiles on our faces

We paint ourselves beige
To match the colours on TV

Obsess over ourselves on repeat
'Why doesn't that look like me?'

Well frankly
Fuck that

When I walk out my door
I want my eyes to sting
With the brightness of *different*

And all those unwanted parts?
I'll take them and cherish each one

Like collecting rare sea shells
I'll worship like the midnight sun

You're stronger, much stronger, than you think

When the darkness descends,
Like an overnight snowdrift
There's no need to cry or wallow
As if greeting an old friend,
Tip your hat instead and
Let the black dog follow

Untitled

13

I want to write a poem about
Self absorbed people
And compare them to sponges
Big sponges, the ones
You have to wrap both hands around
To squeeze out the moisture
Because that's what they do
These people,
They consume everything and
Everyone

But I don't want to give them
Any more of my time

Daffodil

You came into my life like spring,
Full of light and candy sugar

You eased me gently out my burrow
Giggling,
Tickled feet from morning dew

Dragonfly whirring distracts me,
But you hunt me down, planting
Chocolate drizzled kisses

When I scorpion bite
You bumblebee sting

I look down, expecting broken
Roots and weathered heartstring

Instead,
We're surrounded by forget-me-nots

Our ever growing meadow,
Finally happy in my equinox

Someone new

You're like the lingering scent of
Burnt marshmallows and firewood
You find on a forgotten hoodie -
Only good memories

Hindsight

I thought I loved you
And simply didn't like you

Now I know

I fell out of love
And never once liked you

Temporary birthmarks

17

You pepper hickey's along my neckline
Just your way of saying you're mine
Lust drunken on fire flesh,
Tiny strawberries with your finesse

Seatbelt Hugs

You give me seatbelt hugs

Not a light polite embrace
Or a fleeting tight squeeze

But the kind that's powerful
Unstoppable

The kind that allows you to go 100 miles per
hour
Take the leap off the cliff
Plummet, freefall

You give me seatbelt hugs

Not the awkward, half body tap
Or the suffocating chokehold

But the kind that makes you say-
I'm terrified,
Let's do it anyway

You give me seatbelt hugs

I see safety red

I hear the click
I feel the strap across my jaw

Buckled in
Bullet-proof

Lockdown 2

I remember looking in the mirror
Bathroom locked, music playing
I can't let this be my life
Fingers crossed, silently praying

Me Now, Meeting Me Then

I see the wonder in your eyes
You see the pity in mine
I catch the shadows creeping in
But you marvel back, your last lifeline

Like watching a cornered animal,
I can't bear it, turning away
I know just how long it'll take
To embrace my blue jay

Do we let go?
The question is barely a whisper
I taste the torment, the burden
I say, in time
Yes sister

Advise

I've been told that
Time is a fragile thing,
Waste it wisely

Be not afraid

Get hurt and do it all over again
Actually, make sure next time is
Even more deliberate

Take the full force of the wave
Instead of sinking under,
To cushion the blow

In fact,
Stare back at the grinning
Black hole and bare all your teeth
In challenge

Because the people who don't,
Lead doldrum days

They enjoy white noise for background music
Yet there's symphonies out there

Because it's better to have loved and lost
Than to have never loved at all

Because you only have one run up,
To the jump

And if you even slightly hesitate,
You could stumble and plummet

But if you give it everything,
Baby,
You could be flying